The Pueblo
and Their History

by Genevieve St. Lawrence

Content Adviser: Bruce Bernstein, Ph.D.,
Assistant Director for Cultural Resources
National Museum of the American Indian, Smithsonian Institution

Reading Adviser: Rosemary G. Palmer, Ph.D.,
Department of Literacy, College of Education,
Boise State University

COMPASS POINT BOOKS
MINNEAPOLIS, MINNESOTA

Compass Point Books
3109 West 50th Street, #115
Minneapolis, MN 55410

Visit Compass Point Books on the Internet at *www.compasspointbooks.com*
or e-mail your request to *custserv@compasspointbooks.com*

On the cover: Women of the Acoma people of New Mexico bake their bread in a communal outdoor oven shared by a number of families, 1908

Photographs ©: Mary Evans Picture Library, cover, 21; Prints Old & rare, back cover (far left), Library of Congress, back cover, 19, 29; North Wind Picture Archives, 4, 6, 12, 14, 15, 17, 22, 33, 35; Art courtesy George Chacon/photo by Rick Romancito, courtesy *The Taos News*, 7; Kit Breen, 8, 23; Henry Groskinsky/Time Life Pictures/Getty Images, 9; Werner Forman/Art Resource, N.Y., 10; Nancy Carter/North Wind Picture Archives, 16, 32, 41; Peter Stackpole/Time Life Pictures/Getty Images, 18; Corbis, 24; Wolfgang Kaehler/Corbis, 25; Museum of Fine Arts, Houston, Texas, Gift of Miss Ima Hogg/Bridgeman Art Library, 26; George H. H. Huey/Corbis, 27; Museum of New Mexico, #48918, 28; Giovanna Paponetti/Taos Timeline Murals, 31; The Granger Collection, New York, 36; American Stock/Getty Images, 37; AP Photo/Dennis Cook, 38; AP Photo/Albuquerque Journal/Richard Pipes, 39; The Denver Public Library/Western History Department, 40.

Editor: Julie Gassman
Designer/Page Production: Bradfordesign, Inc./Bobbie Nuytten
Photo Researcher: Svetlana Zhurkin
Cartographer: XNR Productions, Inc.
Educational Consultant: Diane Smolinski
Library Consultant: Kathleen Baxter

Managing Editor: Catherine Neitge
Creative Director: Keith Griffin
Editorial Director: Carol Jones

Library of Congress Cataloging-in-Publication Data
St. Lawrence, Genevieve.
 The Pueblo and their history / by Genevieve St. Lawrence.
     p. cm—(We the people)
 Includes bibliographical references and index.
 ISBN 0-7565-1274-3 (hardcover)
 1. Pueblo Indians—History—Juvenile literature. 2. Pueblo Indians—Social life and customs—Juvenile literature. I. Title. II. We the people (Series) (Compass Point Books)
 E99.P9S69 2006
 978.9004'974—dc22   2005003678

TABLE OF CONTENTS

The Pueblo Revolt 4

Who Are the Pueblo? 8

"The Center of Life" 14

The Village Community 17

Pueblo Ceremonies 24

The Spanish Arrive 28

The Struggle for Their Land 35

The Pueblo Today 38

Glossary 42

Did You Know? 43

Important Dates 44

Important People 45

Want to Know More? 46

Index 48

THE PUEBLO REVOLT

Several fast runners left Taos village in New Mexico with a secret message. They followed the banks of the Rio Grande river to the south, crossed desert plateaus, and climbed jagged mountains. The men carried important instructions from Popé, a Pueblo religious leader, to the other Pueblo villages.

Taos was the northernmost Pueblo village.

4

It was August 1680. The runners raced from Taos to Hopi village 300 miles (480 kilometers) west, stopping at more than 70 villages along the way. At each village, they gave the village leader a fiber rope with knots tied in it. The leaders were told to untie one knot each day. When all of the knots were gone, the Pueblo people would revolt against the Spanish government.

The Spanish governor of New Mexico, Antonio de Otermin, heard of a possible rebellion. From his home in Santa Fe, he sent soldiers out to the villages. But it was too late. On August 10, 1680, thousands of Pueblo Indians attacked the Spanish soldiers, settlers, and priests who had forced them to change their way of life.

The Pueblo leaders gave the Spanish people a chance to leave peacefully. Those who did not go were killed. More than 375 Spanish were killed during the revolt. Within a week, the last Spanish people left Santa Fe and headed south toward Mexico. After they left, the Pueblo burned Spanish churches and celebrated the return of their traditional religion.

The Spanish governor's home in Santa Fe was called the Palace of the Governors.

The Spanish had governed the Pueblo for 80 years. They forced many to become Roman Catholics. If a Pueblo religious leader practiced the Pueblo religion, he was beaten or killed. The Spanish also forced the Pueblo to work on Spanish farms and ranches. After long days, they were too tired to work their own fields.

The Pueblo Revolt pushed the Spanish out of New Mexico. But 12 years later, they returned. This time, the

Spanish governor wanted the Pueblo people's help against raiding enemy Indian tribes. So he agreed to allow the Pueblo to practice their religious traditions. In return, most Pueblo villages agreed to keep peace and work with the Spanish.

George Chacon painted "The Pueblo Revolt Began Here–1680" in 1998 as part of a mural program that illustrates Taos Pueblo's history.

WHO ARE THE PUEBLO?

The Pueblo Indians have lived in the southwestern United States for thousands of years. Although rain is more common in the summer, normally the land is very dry. Most water comes from mountain snows that feed large rivers such as the Rio Grande and the Colorado. Summers are hot, and winters can be very cold. Snow covers the high mountains for much of the year.

Less than 20 inches (50.8 centimeters) of rain falls per year in New Mexico, home to most Pueblo villages.

At its peak, Pueblo Bonito in Chaco Canyon had a population of about 1,200.

About 1,000 years ago, ancestors of the Pueblo people built large cities such as Chaco Canyon in present-day New Mexico and Mesa Verde in present-day Colorado. Hundreds of people lived in each of these cities. They constructed elaborate buildings with four or five stories and hundreds of rooms. Each building wall contained hundreds of limestone bricks shaped by workers. The city walls matched the dry, rocky canyon walls around them.

Between 1200 and 1300, the ancient Pueblo people moved away from their great cities. No one knows for sure why they left. Some scientists believe that not enough rain fell in this dry land, so the ancient Pueblo moved to new places that had better sources of water. The people depended on large corn crops for food. They needed water for their crops.

Mesa Verde is home to several ancient villages called cliff dwellings.

10

Some of the ancient Pueblo people built new villages in the Rio Grande Valley in New Mexico. Others built small villages on high mesas in western New Mexico and northern Arizona. By the 1500s, more than 40 Pueblo villages existed.

When the first Spanish soldiers came to the southwestern United States in the 1500s, they saw the Pueblo villages in New Mexico. The villages reminded the soldiers of their towns in Spain. The Spanish gave the Indians the name "Pueblo," which means "town" in Spanish.

Over hundreds of years, each Pueblo village developed its own traditions. Although the cultures of individual villages differ, the Pueblo people still have many things in common with each other and their ancestors. While keeping their own traditions, most villages adopted some Spanish traditions as well. For example, many Pueblo people practice both their native religion and Roman Catholic traditions.

Many Pueblo people adopted some Roman Catholic traditions like Saint's day marches.

The Pueblo Indians are one of the few American Indian tribes that continue to live on their ancient homeland. Today, about 74,000 Pueblo Indians speak four different languages and live in 20 villages in New Mexico and Arizona. The eastern villages are Cochiti, Isleta, Jemez, Nambe, Picuris, Pojoaque, Sandia, San Felipe, San Ildefonso, San Juan, Santa Ana, Santa Clara, Taos, Santo Domingo, Tesuque, and Zia in New Mexico. The western villages include Acoma, Laguna, and Zuni

in New Mexico. Hopi in Arizona is also considered a
Pueblo village, but many Hopi customs vary greatly
from other Pueblo customs.

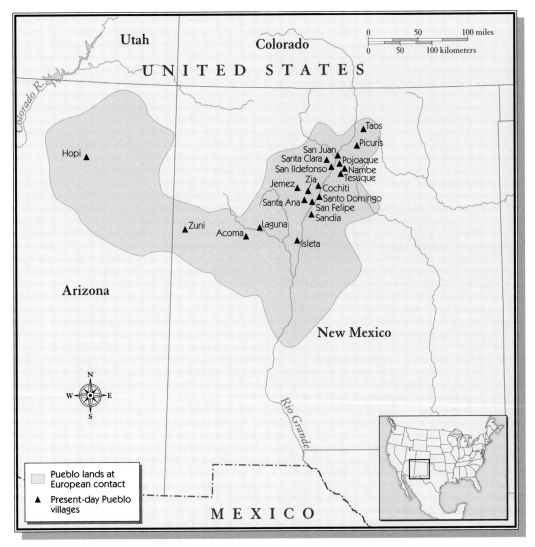

The eastern villages were built along the Rio Grande.

13

"THE CENTER OF LIFE"

Ramson Lomatewama, a Hopi Pueblo poet, learned from his elders that the Pueblo way of life depends on corn. He was taught to "sing to [his] corn" as he sings to his children. "Corn provides us with food. It is the center of life," he said.

Early in the spring, Pueblo families worked together to plant beans, squash, and their most important crop, corn. First, they used a planting stick to dig holes in the hard soil. They dropped several seeds into each hole and later mounded dirt around the

14   *Some villages also raised cotton and melons.*

plants. The mounds gave the plants extra support against the constant wind.

The Pueblo people could not depend on rain to keep their crops watered in this dry land. Instead, they used irrigation systems. The men dug ditches from nearby rivers or lakes to the fields. The river water flowed down these irrigation ditches and kept the fields watered all summer.

Although customs varied from village to village, corn, beans, and squash were raised in all of them.

15

In late summer, the whole family harvested their corn. They roasted fresh corn during the harvest, but they laid most of the ears out in cribs or on rooftops to dry. They stored the dry corn for the coming winter. The Pueblo people used dried corn for more than 30 dishes, such as porridge and thin bread that looked like pancakes. Women and girls spent three to four hours a day grinding the corn for cooking. They used a stone tool set called a mano and metate to crush the corn kernels into flour.

The smaller stone is the mano, and the larger is the metate.

THE VILLAGE COMMUNITY

The Pueblo villages were designed to bring the people together. Each village built houses around a central plaza. This open, flat space gave the Pueblo a place to work together and to meet for dances or ceremonies.

In some villages, houses enclosed the plaza on all sides. The outside walls of the houses acted like a protective fort. There were no windows or doors in the outside walls or on the first floor of each house. This was to keep enemies out of the village and homes.

A ceremonial dance is performed in a Pueblo plaza.

17

The Pueblo built their houses using materials that were easy to come by. They mixed clay with river water and sand to make adobe. They baked these bricks in the sun. After they built the walls with adobe, they plastered the walls and flat roofs with mud.

The houses often had two or three stories. As families grew larger, they built new rooms on top of the original

18   *In later years, the Pueblo added straw to their adobe mixture of clay, sand, and water.*

house. Each story was set back from the one below it, creating rooftop terraces on each level. The families used the roofs to dry food and to cook during the hot summers.

Because Pueblo houses did not have windows or doors on the first floor, people entered a house through a hole in the roof. They used wooden ladders to climb to the roof and down into their home. If enemies came near, they removed the ladders so enemies could not get inside.

A 1903 photo shows the rooftops of each level of the Zuni Pueblo.

19

The different Pueblo families of a village often worked together and shared all they grew, gathered, or hunted. Pueblo men and boys spent most of their day working in the fields. They planted the seeds, hoed the weeds, and harvested the crops. They were also responsible for keeping the irrigation ditches open.

After the harvest, some men went out in parties to hunt large animals like deer, elk, and mountain sheep. Some hunting parties traveled hundreds of miles to hunt buffalo on the Great Plains. Fathers taught their sons to make bows and arrows for hunting. The men carved the animal bones into tools and sewing needles. The meat was dried and saved for winter stews.

Women took care of the house and vegetable gardens. Girls helped their mothers with daily chores and younger children. The women gathered wild onions, seeds, pine nuts, and cactus fruits to eat. They collected yucca roots to use to make soap. The women taught their daughters the best time and places to find wild plants.

A 1908 painting shows a hunter from Taos tracking an animal.

Women spent much of every day preparing food. They dried corn, squash, beans, and vegetables. They ground the corn into cornmeal and fine flour. Women taught their daughters to make clay pots for cooking, carrying water, and storing food. When they were not busy preparing food, the women tanned animal hides for winter clothing and blankets.

Many of the western Pueblo were organized into clans, which were groups of people all related by a common

21

Pueblo pottery is known for its beautiful hand-painted designs.

female ancestor. The oldest woman in the clan was the clan mother and served as head of the household. Clan names came from nature. The Sun Clan, Bear Clan, Lizard Clan, and Corn Clan were found in many villages. Children became members of their mother's clan.

Young adults had to marry someone from a different clan. Young men and women often met at village dances and rabbit hunts. They chose their own marriage partner, but the parents had to approve. After they were married, the young couple moved in with the bride's mother.

Some eastern Pueblos did not use a clan system to organize the village. Instead the people were divided into two groups. Each group had specific responsibilities. For example, San Juan Pueblo was organized into the Summer People and the Winter People. The Summer People were responsible for summer activities, such as growing crops, while the Winter People were responsible for activities such as hunting.

Like San Juan Pueblo, Taos Pueblo is organized into two groups, rather than clans.

23

PUEBLO CEREMONIES

Joe Sando, a Pueblo historian, says, "The Pueblos have no word that translates as 'religion.'" It is a part of everyday life. Religion helps the Pueblo people keep "a harmonious relationship with the world." Land, animals, and people are all connected in the world. The people protect the land and respect all creatures in order to keep the natural balance and ensure they always have food and shelter. The people remember their responsibility to nature in their every action, even simple everyday chores.

The Pueblo people called the important green corn dance ceremony you-pel-lay.

The Pueblo people believe they must thank the spirits of the sky, earth, and animals for good corn crops and successful hunts. They hold ceremonies throughout the year. Every village has corn dance ceremonies. Some also have buffalo dances, deer dances, and rain dances.

Each ceremony includes prayers of thanks and prayers for what they need. Religious leaders learn these prayers from the elders of the village.

Every village has at least one special building for religious ceremonies. This building is called a kiva. Many are circular and are partly under-ground. The Pueblo believe the first humans

A ladder pokes out of a kiva opening.

climbed up into the world from underground. The kiva always has a hole in the floor that represents the opening to the underworld. The kiva is a sacred place. Women are not allowed in most kivas. No young children or strangers are ever allowed inside.

The villages of Hopi and Zuni have unique ceremonies to honor friendly spirits called kachinas. The people believe these spirits live in the mountains for half of the year. For the other six months, the kachinas come to help the people pray for a good corn crop.

A 1933 illustration of different types of kachinas

There are hundreds of different kachinas. Each one represents the spirit of things like animals, lightning, snow, or ancestors. When they dance, men dressed as kachinas often give children small dolls that look like the various kachinas. The dolls help children learn the differences between each kachina.

The Hopi consider Crow Mother to be the mother over all other kachinas.

Although the Pueblo people have lived under Spanish, Mexican, and American governments for more than 400 years, they have been able to preserve their ancient religious ceremonies. Pueblo people pray the same prayers as their ancestors did hundreds of years ago. Their strong religion has helped the Pueblo survive many changes.

27

THE SPANISH ARRIVE

In 1540, a Spanish explorer named Francisco Vásquez de Coronado traveled north from Mexico to search for gold. He brought nearly 300 soldiers with him. He first came to the Pueblo village of Zuni in present-day western New Mexico. Anxious to find gold, Coronado and his soldiers attacked the village. The Pueblo people tried to protect the village with bows and arrows. But the Spanish were better armed and defeated the villagers.

Coronado's attack on the Zuni people is called the Battle of Háwikuh after one of the six pueblos that made up the Zuni village.

Coronado was searching for Cibola, seven cities that according to legend were filled with gold.

Coronado and his soldiers explored the surrounding area to search for gold, using the Zuni village as their base camp. They came to many of the Pueblo villages in their travels. At first the villagers welcomed the visitors. They willingly fed the soldiers and moved out of their homes, so the soldiers had proper shelter. But the soldiers were greedy and rude, and tensions grew. The Pueblo people soon distrusted the Spanish.

After two years, Coronado concluded that there was no gold and returned to Mexico. Though the soldiers had depended on the Pueblo people for food, Coronado reported to the king that the Indians he met were just poor farmers and there was nothing of value in the area. Even so, the king of Spain decided to make New Mexico a Spanish colony.

In 1598, Juan de Oñate led a group of 400 soldiers,

Oñate carved his inscription on El Morro, a landmark near Zuni Pueblo.

Two young Pueblo men peek at Oñate from behind a bush on the left side of this 1999 mural painting by Taos artist Giovanna Paponetti.

missionaries, and families to build the new colony. Oñate led his group up the Rio Grande into northern New Mexico. Most Pueblo went to the mountains to hide from the soldiers. Oñate chose a Pueblo village, sent the remaining native people away, and named it San Gabriel. He claimed the land for Spain and sent the Roman

31

Catholic missionaries to the other Pueblo villages. He served as governor of the colony.

Oñate was a cruel leader. He took what he wanted from the Pueblo and gave their land to Spanish families. The Pueblo who rebelled against the new Spanish government were killed or forced into slavery. Many died from diseases brought by the Spanish, such as smallpox and measles. The Spanish forced many Pueblo to become Roman Catholics. Many pretended to accept the new religion, then practiced their own Pueblo religion in secret.

In 1680, Popé and other Pueblo religious leaders decided to fight back. They had learned to use guns and ride horses. The Pueblo Revolt drove Spanish settlers out of New Mexico. But the Pueblo had learned to depend on some of the things the Spanish brought. They now had cattle, sheep, goats, horses, and chickens. Their way of life had changed.

The Spanish sent a new group of settlers in 1692. Many Pueblo wanted peace and accepted them back. The

Introduced by the Spanish, sheep provided the Pueblo people with meat and wool.

Hopi in Arizona, however, refused to allow missionaries
back into their villages. Some Pueblo people, fearing poor
treatment from the Spanish, fled the area. Some of those

who fled did not return for 40 years.

When the Spanish returned in 1692, they allowed the Pueblo to practice their religion and paid them for their work on Spanish ranches. The Spanish learned to respect Pueblo traditions.

The Spanish brought many new ideas that changed the Pueblo way of life and culture. As one Hopi man said, the white men "did not ask if they could live with us. They just moved in." The Pueblo people did not abandon their old ways, but added new ones. The Pueblo learned to raise cattle, weave wool, and grow wheat from the Spanish.

THE STRUGGLE FOR THEIR LAND

In 1821, Mexico won its independence from Spain, and New Mexico became a Mexican colony. In 1846, the United States declared war on Mexico. The Mexican War (1846–1848) ended when Mexico agreed to give up lands in America's Southwest. The United States paid $15 million for the land that became the states of Texas, California, Arizona, Utah, Nevada, and New Mexico, and parts of Colorado and Wyoming.

The area the United States purchased became known as the Mexican Cession.

While the United States forced many other Indian tribes onto reservations, they did not move the Pueblo people off their land. But when the Americans began to move into New Mexico after the war, the settlers moved onto Pueblo land. The Americans cut timber and built roads and railroads through Pueblo land. They took over rights to water supplies, which are very important in the dry area.

Because the United States did not give them specific reservation land, the Pueblo people have fought for the

A wagon train travels toward Santa Fe, New Mexico.

rights to their land and water supplies, such as lakes and rivers, for the last 150 years. They have taken their battles to the government and the courts.

In some cases, the Pueblo Indians have won. In 1908, the U.S. government took some forested land from the Pueblo village of Taos and created Carson National Forest in New Mexico. This area included Blue Lake, an important water source and a sacred place to the Pueblo. The stream that ran through Taos started at Blue Lake. It took more than 60 years, but in 1970, President Richard Nixon signed a bill to return Blue Lake to the Pueblo. Since then, only Taos Pueblo members are allowed to visit Blue Lake and its surrounding mountains.

Richard Nixon

37

THE PUEBLO TODAY

The Pueblo continue to protect their land and traditions. Each village is an independent nation with its own tribal government, elections, and court system. The tribal governments work to improve the lives of the Pueblo people. For example, the tribal government of Santa Ana Pueblo is trying to create better computer access for the village. Many of the old houses do not have telephone lines. The tribal government is experimenting with wireless connections so that everyone can use the Internet.

Stuwart Paisano, governor of Sandia Pueblo, has worked to improve education and health care.

Some of the Pueblo support their families by farming or raising cattle. But as the population grows, there is not enough land for everyone. Many Pueblo work in nearby New Mexico cities such as Los Alamos, Santa Fe, and Albuquerque. They are doctors, professors, business owners, and teachers.

All Pueblo children speak English and many also know Spanish. The people wish to preserve the traditional Pueblo languages. Pueblo languages are taught in many

Members of San Juan Pueblo work at Pueblo Harvest Foods, a food production business. **39**

villages' elementary schools, preschools, and even a daycare in Cochiti Pueblo.

The Pueblo people are famous for their artistic skills. Pottery, jewelry, painting, and stone carvings bring tourists to the villages in the summer. Many Pueblo women make pottery by hand. Some use designs that were found on pottery at Chaco Canyon. Artists use colorful turquoise stone in silver jewelry. Zuni artists carve turquoise into tiny animals. Each Pueblo village is known for its pottery, beadwork, or jewelry styles.

Religion continues to be an important part of daily life. Most tribal governments protect the sacred traditions of the villages. As more young people move away to find

Pueblo potter Maria Martinez was famous worldwide.

jobs, the Pueblo elders fear the young will not learn their native language and the prayers of their ancestors.

But the young people still come home for special ceremonies and dances. They remember their connection to the land. As Rina Swentzell, a Pueblo historian says, "What we are told as children is that when people walk on the land, they leave their breath wherever they go. So, wherever we walk, that particular spot on earth never forgets us."

Young Pueblo people are dressed to perform the traditional Rainbow Dance.

41

GLOSSARY

adobe—brick made of clay and water and dried in the sun

ceremonies—traditional prayers or dances used to celebrate a special occasion

cribs—small buildings in which corn or other grains are kept

harmonious—balanced; equal in give and take

irrigation—a way of bringing water to fields through canals or ditches

kachinas—friendly spirits; also, dancers imitating a spirit

kiva—underground room used for special ceremonies

mesas— broad hills with flat tops and steep sides

missionaries—people who travel to new lands to teach a religion

plaza—public square or open space

rebellion—a fight against a government or ruler

revolt—an uprising against a government or authority

tanned—made animal hide into leather

DID YOU KNOW?

- The ancient Pueblo homes at Chaco Canyon and Mesa Verde are the first "apartment" buildings of North America.

- The Pueblo homeland is often called the Four Corners. This is the region where the states of Utah, Colorado, New Mexico, and Arizona meet.

- Ancient Pueblo people carved pictures, which tell us about their lives, on stones. These petroglyphs can be seen at Petroglyph National Monument in Albuquerque, New Mexico.

- Traders brought corn and squash seeds to North America from Mexico at least 2,000 years ago.

- Turquoise stone is only found in a few places in the world, including Nevada and New Mexico. It has been an important religious and trade item for the Pueblo.

IMPORTANT DATES

Timeline

800	The ancient Pueblo build large cities in present-day New Mexico and Colorado.
1200	The ancient Pueblo move to the Rio Grande Valley in New Mexico and mesas in northeastern Arizona.
1540	Spanish explorer Francisco Vásquez de Coronado comes to the Pueblo lands to look for gold.
1598	Juan de Oñate founds the first Spanish colony in New Mexico near the San Juan Pueblo.
1680	Pueblo leaders rebel against the Spanish and drive them out of New Mexico.
1821	Mexico declares independence from Spain.
1848	The United States claims New Mexico after the Mexican War.
1912	New Mexico becomes the 47th state.
1948	The Pueblo win the right to vote.
1970	President Nixon signs a bill to return Blue Lake to the Taos Pueblo.
1992	Taos Pueblo is recognized by the World Heritage Society for its historical and cultural uniqueness.

IMPORTANT PEOPLE

FRANCISCO VÁSQUEZ DE CORONADO (1510?–1554)
Spanish explorer who led 300 soldiers into Pueblo land in search of gold

MARIA MONTOYA MARTINEZ (1887–1980)
Artist from San Ildefonso Pueblo who developed a unique style of pottery that is found in museums all over the world

JUAN DE OÑATE (1550?–1626?)
Spanish explorer who established the colony of New Mexico and served as its governor

POPÉ (1630?–1690?)
Religious leader from San Juan Pueblo who helped to organize and lead the Pueblo Revolt of 1680

JOE SANDO (1923–)
Historian and author from Jemez Pueblo who wrote an important book, Pueblo Nations: Eight Centuries of Pueblo Indian History, *about Pueblo history and culture*

WANT TO KNOW MORE?

At the Library

Bial, Raymond. *The Pueblo.* New York: Benchmark Books, 2000.

Bishop, Amanda. *Life in a Pueblo.* New York: Crabtree Publishing, 2003.

Englar, Mary. *The Pueblo: Southwestern Potters.* Mankato, Minn.: Blue Earth Books, 2003.

Rosinsky, Natalie. *The Hopi.* Minneapolis: Compass Point Books, 2004.

Vivian, R. Gwinn, and Margaret Anderson. *Chaco Canyon.* New York: Oxford University Press, 2002.

On the Web

For more information on the *Pueblo*, use FactHound

to track down Web sites related to this book.

1. Go to *www.facthound.com*

2. Type in a search word related to this book
   or this book ID: 0756512743

3. Click on the *Fetch It* button.

Your trusty FactHound will fetch the best Web sites for you!

On the Road

Chaco Canyon

Chaco Culture National

Historical Park

P.O. Box 220

Nageezi, NM 87037-0220

505/786-7014

To see the architecture of the 1,000-

year-old Pueblo city

Indian Pueblo Cultural Center

2401 12th St. NW

Albuquerque, NM 87104

505/843-7270 or 800/766-4405

To see historical artifacts, photo-

graphs, and art of the 19 New

Mexico pueblos

Look for more We the People books about this era:

The Alamo

The Arapaho and Their History

The Battle of the Little Bighorn

The Buffalo Soldiers

The California Gold Rush

The Cherokee and Their History

The Chumash and Their History

The Creek and Their History

The Erie Canal

Great Women of Pioneer America

Great Women of the Old West

The Iroquois and Their History

The Lewis and Clark Expedition

The Louisiana Purchase

The Mexican War

The Ojibwe and Their History

The Oregon Trail

The Pony Express

The Powhatan and Their History

The Santa Fe Trail

The Sioux and Their History

The Trail of Tears

The Transcontinental Railroad

The Wampanoag and Their History

The War of 1812

A complete list of We the People titles is available on our Web site:
www.compasspointbooks.com

47

INDEX

Arizona, 11, 12, 13, 33, 35
art, 40

Blue Lake, 37

California, 35
Carson National Forest, 37
ceremonies, 17, 24–26, 27, 41
Chaco Canyon, New Mexico, 9, 40
children, 20, 21, 22, 26, 27, 39
clans, 21–22
Cochiti Pueblo, 12, 40
Colorado, 9, 35
Colorado River, 8
corn, 10, 14, 16, 21, 25, 26
Coronado, Francisco Vásquez de,
    28, 29, 30

dance, 17, 22, 25, 27, 40

farming, 6, 10, 14–16, 20, 23, 34,
    38
food, 10, 14, 16, 19, 20, 21, 24

gold, 28, 30

Hopi village, 5, 13, 26, 33
houses, 17–19
hunting, 20, 22, 23, 25

irrigation, 15, 20

kachinas, 26–27
kivas, 25–26

languages, 12, 39–40, 41
Lomatewama, Ramson, 14

mano tool, 16
marriage, 22–23
men, 15, 20, 27
Mesa Verde, Colorado, 9
metate tool, 16
Mexican War, 35
missionaries, 31–32, 33

Nevada, 35
New Mexico, 4, 5, 6–7, 11, 12, 28,
    31, 32, 35, 36, 39
Nixon, Richard, 37

Oñate, Juan de, 30–32
Otermin, Antonio de, 5

plazas, 17
Popé (religious leader), 4, 32
Pueblo Revolt, 5–6, 32

religion, 5, 6, 7, 11, 24–27, 32, 34,

40–41
Rio Grande, 4, 8, 30
Rio Grande Valley, 11
Roman Catholicism, 6, 11, 31–32

San Gabriel, New Mexico, 31
San Juan Pueblo, 12, 23
Sando, Joe, 24
Santa Ana Pueblo, 12, 38
Santa Fe, New Mexico, 5, 39
settlers, 5, 32, 33, 36
Spain, 5–7, 11, 28–34, 35
Summer People, 23
Swentzell, Rina, 41

Taos village, 4, 12, 37
Texas, 35
tribal governments, 38, 40

Utah, 35

villages, 4, 5, 11, 12–13, 17, 25, 26,
    28, 29, 31, 33, 37, 38, 40

Winter People, 23
women, 20–21, 22, 26, 40
Wyoming, 35

Zuni village, 13, 26, 28, 29, 40

About the Author

Genevieve St. Lawrence is a freelance author of more than 30 nonfiction books for children. A graduate of Gustavus Adolphus College in St. Peter, Minnesota, she lives and writes in Minnesota.